SPEED!
MOTORCYCLES

Jenifer Corr Morse

WITHDRAWN

BLACKBIRCH PRESS, INC.
WOODBRIDGE, CONNECTICUT

To Christopher P. Morse
Thanks for all your help.
–JCM

Published by Blackbirch Press, Inc.
260 Amity Road
Woodbridge, CT 06525
Web site: www.blackbirch.com
e-mail: staff@blackbirch.com

Printed in Belgium

10 9 8 7 6 5 4 3 2 1

Photo Credits
Cover (top), pages 6–7, 16–17: courtesy Kawasaki Motors Corporation; cover (bottom right), pages 1, 10–11, 22–23: courtesy Yamaha Motor Corporation; cover (bottom left), back cover (top), pages 15, 21: Corel Corporation; back cover (bottom), pages 13 (bottom), 18 (top), 20 (top): PhotoDisc; pages 4–5, 9: Moto Point, Inc.; pages 12, 13 (top), 20 (bottom): courtesy Suzuki; pages 14, 18 (bottom): courtesy Honda.

Library of Congress Cataloging-in-Publication Data
Morse, Jenifer Corr.
    Motorcycles / by Jenifer Morse.
       p. cm. — (Speed!)
Includes bibliographical references and index.
    ISBN 1-56711-470-9 (hardcover)
    1. Motorcycles, Racing—Juvenile literature. [1. Motorcycles, Racing.] I. Title II. Speed! (Woodbridge, Conn.)
TL442 .M67 2001
629.227'5—dc21
                                                00-012853

Contents

Bimota YB-11

Produces a peak 145 horsepower

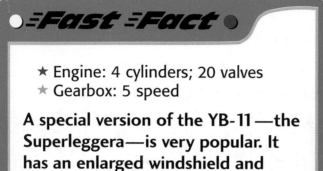

●≡Fast ≡Fact●

★ Engine: 4 cylinders; 20 valves
★ Gearbox: 5 speed

A special version of the YB-11—the Superleggera—is very popular. It has an enlarged windshield and comes in blue and gray.

The sleek and sporty Bimota YB-11 is the fifth-fastest production motorcycle in the world. It can reach a top speed of 175 miles (282 km) per hour. That's about three times the speed limit on most local highways!

This super sleek sports bike has a maximum 145 horsepower and a powerful 4 cylinder Yamaha Thunder Ace engine (better known in the U.S. as the FZR 1000) with a

A lightweight body and a powerful engine make the Bimota a super accelerator.

liquid coolant. There are five valves in each engine cylinder. The YB-11 comes fully equipped with many state-of-the-art features, such as a digital electronic ignition. The bike also features 4 1.5-inch (38-mm) carburetors and holds about 3.9 gallons (15 l) of fuel.

The Bimota has a light-weight aluminum frame and weighs about 403 pounds (183 kg). The YB-11's low overall weight and powerful engine enable it to accelerate quickly and take turns easily. The heavy duty front and rear suspension and excellent shock absorbers keep the ride especially smooth. All these special features do not come cheap: the Bimota's price tag is about $20,300.

The sporty YB-11 can reach a top speed of 175 miles (282 km) per hour.

Kawasaki ZRX1200R

Muscle bike with a huge engine

Unlike the sleek sports bikes that have streamlined bodywork covering their machinery, the Kawasaki ZRX1200R is an "open class muscle bike." That means the engine area is exposed. Muscle bikes focus more on the size and power of the engine than on the aerodynamic outer shell.

The ZRX1200R engine is huge, measuring 1,164 cubic centimeters. Motorcycle pistons—like car pistons—push up and down in each cylinder to produce power for the engine. The more cylinders a bike has, the more powerful it is. The 2001 ZRX1200R features high-tech aluminum cylinders that are electroplated to transfer heat quickly and produce more power. With all its cylinders pumping full throttle, this muscle bike can reach a top speed of 160 miles (257 km) an hour.

The ZRX1200R has a huge, exposed engine.

"Muscle bikes" focus on power more than aerodynamics.

The front and rear suspension on a vehicle determine how smooth or bumpy the ride will be. The suspension system is made up of many small springs that absorb most of the vibrations that would rattle the driver. Both the front and back suspension of the ZRX1200R are fully adjustable so the rider can set the shock absorbers to his or her preference.

Fast Fact

★ Engine: 4 cylinders; 16 valves

You can buy the Kawasaki ZRX1200R for about $8,000. It comes in candy lime green and vivid purple mica, as well as in black pearl and metallic blue violet.

Bimota SB8R

Can reach a top speed of 180 miles (290 km) an hour

The SB8R is Bimota's fastest motorcycle. It can reach a top speed of 180 miles (290 km) an hour, which makes it the fourth-fastest production motorcycle in the world. In fact, the SB8R was designed mainly to compete in Superbike races.

The SB8R is a solid motorcycle with enough power to outrun almost any other bike.

With a powerful 4-stroke, Suzuki TL1000R twin-cylinder engine, the SB8R can deliver 145 horsepower. The SB8R has large bores (the bore is the part of the engine where the piston moves up and down. Larger bores can accommodate larger pistons, and that means more power). This six-speed motorcycle also has an electronic inductive ignition and a 13-volt battery. It has a special electronic injection system for fueling, and can carry up to 6.3 gallons (24 l) of gas.

The SB8R is built to be solid—its frame consists of two aluminum alloy beams and carbon fiber plates. Even with its solid frame, the SB8R only weighs 394 pounds (179 kg), which makes it easy to maneuver through curvy roads and hairpin turns. Designed with super-sleek aerodynamic features that prevent excess drag, this bike can reach speeds that put it near the front of the pack.

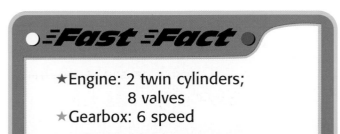

Fast Fact

★Engine: 2 twin cylinders; 8 valves
★Gearbox: 6 speed

The SB8R first became available in 1998. Today it sells for about $23,600.

Yamaha YZF-R1

A super lightweight speedster

Although the Yamaha YZF-R1 was first introduced in 1998, it is virtually a brand new machine today. The super-quick motorcycle underwent more than 150 component changes for the 2000 model. It is able to reach a top speed of 175 miles (281 km) an hour.

The power behind the new YZF-R1 is its impressive engine which is compact, lightweight, and produces a maximum of 150 horsepower. The six-speed transmission transfers the power between gears for immediate acceleration. A special feature—the Exhaust Ultimate Powervalve (EXUP) monitors—also adjust exhaust flow for optimum performance and acceleration.

Hollow bolts and ultra-light titanium help to keep the YZF-R1 light and fast.

The YZF-R1 can reach a top speed of 175 miles (281 km) per hour.

One aspect that makes the YZF-R1 so speedy is its super low weight of 385 pounds (175 kg). Many of the bike's parts were designed specifically to keep the bike's weight low. The ultra-light titanium muffler and the hollow bolts and fasteners are just two examples. The aerodynamic shape of the YZF-R1 also enhances its speed. The headlight profile, fuel tank, and tail section were specially designed by computers in high-tech wind tunnels. The finished product allows air to flow around the bike, which reduces drag and increases speed.

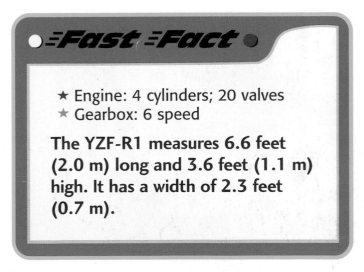

● **Fast Fact** ●

★ Engine: 4 cylinders; 20 valves
★ Gearbox: 6 speed

The YZF-R1 measures 6.6 feet (2.0 m) long and 3.6 feet (1.1 m) high. It has a width of 2.3 feet (0.7 m).

Suzuki GSX1300R Hayabusa

The world's fastest production motorcycle

Cruising along at a top speed of 186 miles (299 km) an hour, the Suzuki GSX1300R Hayabusa is the world's fastest production motorcycle. The name Hayabusa refers to one of the fastest species of falcons that live in Japan. It is rumored that the idea for this speedy bike was born after an engineer saw the Hayabusa cut through the air at around 175 miles (282 km) per hour.

The world's fastest production bike can reach a top speed of 186 miles (299 km) per hour.

While designing the
GSX1300R, Suzuki engineers
kept the aerodynamics of the Hayabusa in mind. They
wanted to keep the motorcycle as streamlined as possible so it would
not have any excess
drag (loss of speed due
to wind force). To
accomplish this aerody-
namic goal, the design
elements in the front of
the bike include a
unique stacked head-
light and compact front
turn signals.

The GSX1300R gets
its power from a liquid-cooled, inline four-cylinder dual overhead cam
engine. With its 6-speed transmission, this bike can reach a peak 172
horsepower. It has won several major awards, including Motorcycle of
the Year and Best Superbike. The GSX1300R
retails for around $10,500.

● ⸗Fast ⸗Fact ●

★ Engine: 4 cylinders; 16 valves
★ Gearbox: 6 speed

The GSX1300R Hayabusa was designed to replace the GSX-R1100. It has the smallest amount of drag of any motorcycle in its class.

Honda RC51

A streetbike prototype

Although the Honda RC51 was designed as a production motorcycle, racing is probably not far in its future. In fact, this sporty machine was developed to be a prototype for Honda's upcoming Superbike racing entries. Recent tests show that this bike can reach a top speed of 170 miles (273 km) per hour.

Equipped with a 6-speed transmission and an engine that produces 126 horsepower, the RC51 is one of the sportiest motorcycles around.

The RC51 is a production bike that's fast enough for the race track.

The Honda 500cc Grand Prix racing bike has been one of the company's best performers.

Even though the engine is fairly large, the bike isn't too heavy. The RC51 weighs in at only 432 pounds (196 kg), which helps to keep it swift and agile.

The sturdy 2001 RC51 is built around an aluminum frame that weighs just 25.8 pounds (11.7 kg). The specially designed Honda Multi-Action System cartridge fork controls the damping settings. (This allows the rider to easily adjust the shocks to the appropriate stiffness depending on the type of riding he or she will do.) In general, the shocks are much stiffer during motorcycle racing than they are during normal street driving.

=Fast =Fact

★ Engine: 2 cylinders; 8 valves
★ Gearbox: 6 speed

The RC51 premiered in April 2000. People were excited about the bike before it was even available; many customers had to wait until the next production year to buy one because the stock was so low. The RC51 retails for just $10,000.

Super lightweight parts made of magnesium have made the ZX-6R much faster and more agile.

Kawasaki Ninja ZX-6R

High power and low weight combine for speed

The Kawasaki Ninja ZX-6R is one of the most powerful motorcycles in its class. A compact but powerful engine means the ZX-6R can reach a top speed of 169 miles (272 km) per hour.

Recent redesigns reduced the ZX-6R's overall weight and increased its speed dramatically. Many parts are now made of lightweight magnesium instead of heavier aluminum.

One special feature of the ZX-6R is its very efficient fuel delivery system. The narrow valve angles of the intake tract provide a direct path for the gas to reach the engine. The Twin Ram Air intake system also improves the bike's performance. Large ducts at the front of the motorcycle feed cool air to the engine as the bike's speed rises.

=Fast =Fact

★ Engine: 4 cylinders; 16 valves
★ Gearbox: 6 speed

The Kawasaki Throttle Responsive Ignition Control (K-TRIC) has a throttle position sensor that tells the ignition control how hard the engine is working. A micro-computer can then determine the best ignition timing for more power and better gas mileage.

Honda CBR1100XX

Reaches a top speed of 181 miles (291 km) an hour

The Honda CBR1100XX—also known as the Blackbird—can cruise along at a top speed of 181 miles (291 km) per hour. That's as fast as some of the world's fastest production cars! Super acceleration and power make the CBR1100XX the third-fastest production motorcycle in the world.

The Blackbird is the world's third-fastest production motorcycle.

The bike's highly aero-dynamic design is one feature that allows it to move so fast. To develop the most efficient design, Honda engineers put the bike through hundreds of hours of wind-tunnel testing. To avoid any excess wind resistance, they designed the motorcycle with a low overall frontal area and a very sharp nose that cuts through the air.

A large liquid cooled engine and six-speed transmission give the Blackbird its pure power. A specially created dual-shaft engine balancer system almost completely eliminates high-frequency engine vibration and keeps the ride smooth. The carburetor also features electric fuel injection.

Fast Fact

★ Engine: 4 cylinders; 16 valves
★ Gearbox: 6 speed

The CBR1100XX has one of the lowest drag measurements of any bike its size. At the same time, the front area is able to provide solid wind protection to the driver.

Suzuki GSX-R600

Great performance on the street and the track

The Suzuki GSX-R600 is a multipurpose bike that excels on both the racetrack and the highway. The bike's excellent suspension is the key to its flexibility. Both the front and rear suspension are fully adjustable, allowing the rider to adapt the motorcycle to handle almost any environment. The engine design of the GSX-R600 also allows the bike to perform superbly in many kinds of settings. The compact engine leaves room for

Super control and adjustable suspension make the GSX-R600 a highly flexible speedster.

The Suzuki drag racer is another star on the racetrack.

a 54.5-inch (139-cm) wheel base and keeps the bike to a low overall weight of 384 pounds (174 kg). These two features give the rider excellent control on both twisty roads and racetrack curves.

Even though the liquid cooled engine is compact, it is still very powerful. In competition, the engine's 4 large 1.4-inch (36-mm) carburetors and short-stroke design (short distance for the pistons to move) produce high-end performance.

≡*Fast ≡Fact* •

★Engine: 4 cylinders; 16 valves
★Gearbox: 6 speed

The GSX-R600 comes in three color combinations—blue and white, yellow and black, and blue and black. This motorcycle retails for about $8,000.

The Suzuki 500cc racing bike is a top performer on the track.

Yamaha YZF600R

A powerful bike for everyday driving

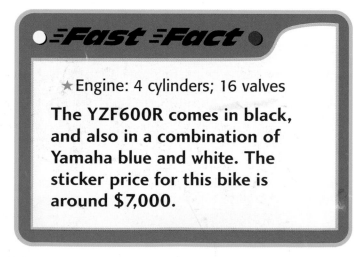

The Yamaha YZF600R is proof that a motorcycle can generate a great deal of power for high-performance racing, and still be comfortable enough to ride around town for everyday use. This middleweight supersport bike can reach a top speed of 155 miles (249 km) per hour.

The liquid-cooled Genesis engine gives the bike the right amount of power for both aggressive sports riding and everyday driving. A light, compact engine helps keep the bike's overall weight down to a relatively low 416 pounds (188 kg). Lightweight pistons help to keep the engine light and increase its throttle response. The ram-air-style intake valve has a central duct below the headlight to draw pressure-cooled air into the engine. The fully adjustable front and rear suspension give the operator excellent control of the ride.

> ## Fast Fact
>
> ★ Engine: 4 cylinders; 16 valves
>
> **The YZF600R comes in black, and also in a combination of Yamaha blue and white. The sticker price for this bike is around $7,000.**

The YZF600R is one of the sleekest bikes around. Its components and bodywork were designed to cut through the air with the least possible amount of drag and wind resistance. At the same time, its tall windshield protects the rider from the powerful forces of rushing air and airborne debris.

The sleek design of the YZF600R creates an aerodynamic shape that cuts through the wind with ease.

Glossary

carburetor: the part of an engine where air and gasoline mix
electroplated: covered with a special plate that conducts heat
muffler: a device that reduces the noise made by an engine
piston: a disk or cylinder that moves back and forth in a large cylinder
throttle: a valve in a vehicle's engine that opens to let steam, fuel, or fuel and air
  flow into it, thereby controlling the speed

For More Information

Books

Graham, Ian S. *Motorcycles* (Built for Speed). Chatham, NJ: Raintree/Steck
  Vaughn, 1998.
Graham, Ian S. *Motorcycles* (Worldwise). Danbury, CT: Franklin Watts, Inc., 1998.
Raby, Philip. *Motorbikes: The Need for Speed.* Minneapolis, MN: Lerner
  Publications Company, 1999.

Web Site

Kawasaki
Find more information about and photos of Kawasaki motorcycles—
www.kawasaki.com/index.html.

Index